THE DIAGRAMMING DICTIONARY

The Diagramming Dictionary uses example sentences from the ***Grammar for the Well-Trained Mind* series** by Susan Wise Bauer.

ABOUT *GRAMMAR FOR THE WELL-TRAINED MIND*

Core Instructor Text

Scripted lessons make it possible for any parent or teacher to use the program effectively.

Step-by-step instruction takes students from the most basic concepts through advanced grammatical concepts. This instructor text is used for all four years of the *GFTWTM* series.

Student Workbooks

Each workbook allows students to practice the grammar they have learned. Diagramming exercises reinforce the rules and help technical and visual learners to understand and use the English language effectively. Each step of the diagramming process is illustrated and thoroughly explained to the student. Examples and exercises are drawn from great works of literature, as well as from well-written nonfiction texts in science, mathematics, and the social sciences. Regular review is built into each year of work.

Purple Workbook (2017)
Red Workbook (2018)
Blue Workbook (2019)
Yellow Workbook (2021)

Keys to Student Workbooks

Each Key to the workbooks provides not only answers, but also explanations for the parent/teacher.

Key to Purple Workbook (2017)
Key to Red Workbook (2018)
Key to Blue Workbook (2019)
Key to Yellow Workbook (2021)

The Grammar Guidebook

Capable of accompanying the *Grammar for the Well-Trained Mind* program or standing on its own as a lifelong reference companion, *The Grammar Guidebook* assembles into one handy reference work all of the principles that govern the English language—from basic definitions ("A noun is the name of a person, place, thing, or idea") through advanced sentence structure and analysis. Each rule is illustrated with examples drawn from great literature, along with classic and contemporary works of science, history, and mathematics.

THE DIAGRAMMING DICTIONARY

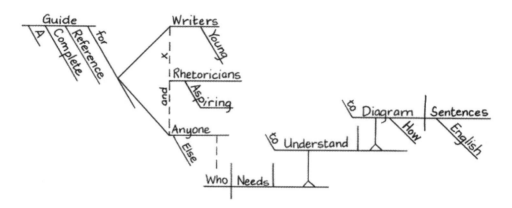

By Jessica Otto and Susan Wise Bauer

Diagrams by Patty Rebne

WELL-TRAINED MIND PRESS

Publisher's Cataloging-In-Publication Data
(Prepared by The Donahue Group, Inc.)

Names: Otto, Jessica, author. | Bauer, Susan Wise, author. | Rebne, Patty,
illustrator.
Title: The diagramming dictionary / by Jessica Otto and Susan Wise Bauer ;
diagrams by Patty Rebne.
Description: [Charles City, Virginia] : Well-Trained Mind Press, [2019] | "A
Complete Reference Guide for Young Writers, Aspiring Rhetoricians, and
Anyone Else Who Needs to Understand How to Diagram English Sentences." |
Designed in conjunction with the Grammar for the Well-Trained Mind series.
| Includes index. | Interest age level: 11 and up. | Audience: Middle and high
school instructors.
Identifiers: ISBN 9781945841385 | ISBN 9781945841392 (ebook)
Subjects: LCSH: English language--Grammar--Dictionaries--Juvenile literature.
| English language--Sentences--Dictionaries--Juvenile literature. | English
language--Rhetoric--Dictionaries--Juvenile literature. | CYAC: English
language--Grammar--Dictionaries. | English language--Sentences--Dictionaries.
| English language--Rhetoric--Dictionaries.
Classification: LCC LB1631 .O88 2019 (print) | LCC LB1631 (ebook) | DDC
428.00712--dc23

For a list of corrections, please visit www.welltrainedmind.com/corrections

Cover design by Mike Fretto

TABLE OF CONTENTS

FOREWORD

Once you learn how to diagram sentences, you'll *really* understand how English works.

To diagram a sentence, you have to know more than just memorized definitions of parts of speech. You have to know how those parts of speech work together to produce meaning. And that makes you a better writer.

Think of it this way: Anyone can walk into a building and point out the bathroom, hallway, stairs, or kitchen. But that doesn't explain how and why the building functions. Only a blueprint will reveal the true underlying structure—the structure that makes the building functional.

You can wander through a building without ever looking at the blueprint, and you can be a contented reader without ever sketching out a sentence diagram. But to design a useful building, or to put together an effective sentence, you need a deeper knowledge. You need to know how the parts all fit together.

Diagramming doesn't just deepen your understanding of the English language; it also gives you a diagnostic tool to figure out whether your own sentences are weak or strong, and why.

Consider the following balanced and beautiful sentence, from nineteenth-century poet Gerard Manley Hopkins:

> *Our prayer and God's grace are like two buckets in a well; while the one ascends, the other descends.*

Read it out loud, and then read the following student sentence out loud. Listen to the difference.

> *In* Pride and Prejudice, *her mother's bad manners and wishing to get married made Elizabeth discontent.*

The second sentence makes sense—but it isn't a pretty sentence. It's weak and clunky. Why?

Time to diagram!

In the Hopkins sentence, the subject and verb of the first independent clause are diagrammed like this:

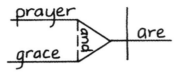

The second sentence also has a compound subject and single verb:

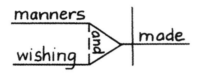

But in the second sentence, the two subjects are two different kinds of words. "Manners" is a noun, while "wishing" is a gerund—a verb form used as a noun. Words which occupy parallel places on a diagram should take the same form—as in the Hopkins sentence, where "prayer" and "grace" are both nouns.

Now you know why the first sentence soars, and the second one thuds.

Here's another example. Without diagramming, can you figure out why the following sentence doesn't work?

> *In addition to the city, Theodore Dreiser's society is depicted in its people.*

It's an awkward, ugly sentence. Diagramming it shows why.

Here are the subject (society) and verb (is depicted), diagrammed on a simple subject/verb line, with the prepositional phrase "in its people" diagrammed underneath the verb (it is acting as an adverb, because it answers the question "how").

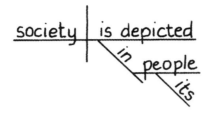

But where should "In addition to the city" go?

It doesn't seem to fit anywhere. Are the society and city both depicted? (If so, what's the difference?) Is the society depicted in its people or in its city? (Neither is particularly clear.)

If you can't put it on the diagram, it doesn't belong in the sentence. The author of this sentence doesn't exactly know what Dreiser is depicting, and he's hoping to sneak his fuzzy comprehension past the reader.

Here's something important to keep in mind: The examples in this Dictionary are neat and tidy, but your diagrams don't need to be. Successful diagramming takes a lot of erasing and rewriting and running off the edge of the paper. Good diagrams often have scribbled-out parts and corrections. Your diagrams don't have to look like architectural plans. They can look like messy pencil sketches or works of art.

Here are a few suggestions:

Don't diagram in pen! Your first approach to the sentence will probably need fixing as you progress on. Use a soft lead pencil, nice and sharp, and be sure to keep a separate eraser on hand, because you *will* need to erase and redraw as you go.

Don't diagram on paper with regular ruled lines—use either plain sheets of paper, or else graph paper (that's for diagrammers who really like all of their lines to be tidy). If you do use graph paper, blue lines are better than black, because you can see what is pencil and what is grid line.

If your diagram runs off the edge of the page, just tape another piece of paper to the first one. You don't have to redo the whole thing!

Lines don't have to be perfectly straight! You can use a ruler or triangle if you *really* want to, but as long as the different parts of the diagram connect to each other in the right places, don't worry about how much the lines twist and turn.

Here's Susan's original sketch of the following sentence (from *The Autobiography of Benjamin Franklin*):

> *In this manner we lay all night, with very little rest; but the wind abating the next day, we made a shift to reach Amboy before night, having been thirty hours on the water, without victuals, or any drink but a bottle of dirty rum, the water we sailed on being salt.*

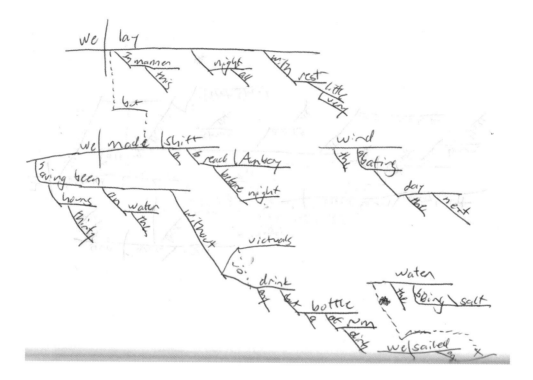

Those are definitely not straight lines. But now look how neat and tidy the graphic design version of this sentence is.

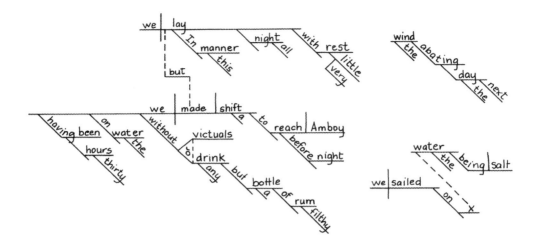

Both diagrams are correct! When you're diagramming, pay more attention to the functions and relationships shown, not the shape or tidiness of the diagram. As long as the lines are connecting the right words, the diagram is fine.

And those lines can connect the right words in different ways. Here's a sentence from the O. Henry short story "The Cop and the Anthem":

> *Through one violet-stained window a soft light glowed, where, no doubt, the organist loitered over the keys, making sure of his mastery of the coming Sabbath anthem.*

When you diagram this, it's important that a dotted line connect "light" to "where" ("where" is a relative adverb linking the descriptive clause to the subject of the main clause). But that line can go in any direction. Here's one way to do it:

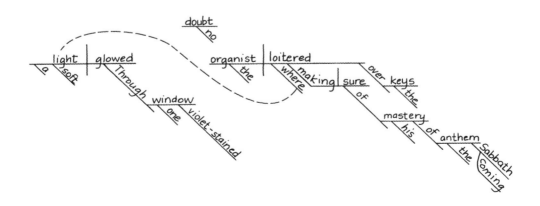

But a left-handed student would probably prefer to make the diagram up-and-down, rather than wide, so that she doesn't leave smudges on the independent clause.

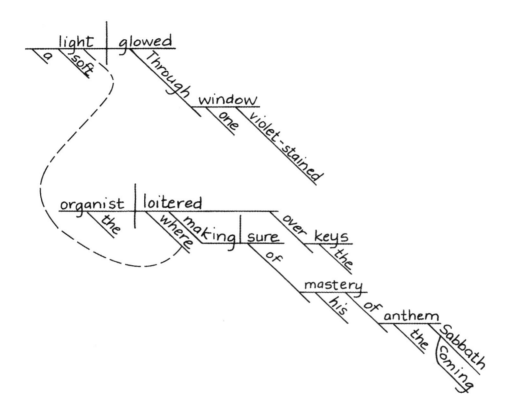

Sometimes, small elements of diagrams are important. For example, prepositions are diagrammed on a slanting line, with their objects on a horizontal line that branches off the slant just before it ends, so that the slanting line has a little tail. But infinitives are diagrammed on a bending line with no tail. This is important because all infinitives begin with "to," but "to" can also be a preposition. The diagram shows you what kind of word "to" is.

preposition   part of an infinitive

to store
the

to dream

But does it matter whether the line you diagram your present participle on curves to the right or has a sharp angle? Absolutely not, because it's perfectly clear that the word is a present participle.

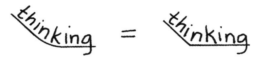

thinking = thinking

So don't get overwhelmed by making your diagrams somehow "perfect." Do your best to represent the relationship between the words in a way that's helpful to you. And remember: Diagramming isn't an arcane assignment designed to torture young writers. Instead, it forces them to clarify their thinking, fix their sentences, and put grammar to use in the service of writing—which is, after all, what grammar is for.

BEFORE WE BEGIN

Before we begin, let's review the most basic skill in diagramming: how to diagram a subject and predicate!

First, draw a horizontal line. Next, divide the line in half with a vertical line. Make sure your vertical line goes all the way through the horizontal line. This vertical line divides everything in the subject from everything in the predicate.

$$\underline{\text{subject}} \mid \underline{\text{predicate}}$$

The simple subject goes to the left of the vertical line. The simple predicate goes to the right of the vertical line. Everything in the complete subject will attach itself to the diagram on the left. Everything in the complete predicate will attach itself to the right. Keep that in mind for everything you diagram! In the examples that follow, every simple subject is underlined once, and every simple predicate is underlined twice. Some sentences contain more than one subject and predicate, especially if they are made up of multiple clauses.

In each sample sentence, you will see that some of the words are in green. That indicates the part of the sentence we are focusing on in that particular example.

Note: When you are diagramming, always keep the capitalization of the original! (So be sure to capitalize the first word of the sentence on your diagram.) Punctuation does not go on diagrams (although sometimes you may represent punctuation with an *x*).

PART I: HOW TO DIAGRAM THE SIMPLE SUBJECT AND SIMPLE PREDICATE OF A SENTENCE

IA. Simple subjects

1. **Common nouns** as subjects: When a common noun is used as the subject of a sentence, put it on the subject line.

The <u>book</u> <u>is</u> open.

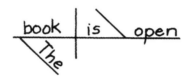

2. **The understood you** as subject: In a command (imperative) sentence, the subject is understood to be "you." It is placed in parentheses on the subject line of the diagram to show that it does not appear in the sentence itself.

<u>Close</u> the book.

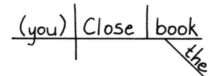

1

3. **Pronouns** as subjects: A personal pronoun is often the subject of a sentence and is diagrammed exactly as the noun it is replacing would be diagrammed.

You did a good job today.

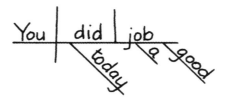

4. **Compound nouns** as subjects: A compound noun can be two separate words, two words joined by a hyphen, or two words that have been combined into one. A compound noun is always kept together on the same space of the diagram.

Unfortunate mix-ups happen.

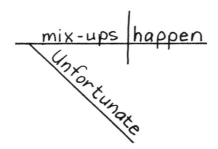

Your desk lamp illuminates.

5. Compound subjects: A compound subject consists of two or more subjects joined by a conjunction. A compound subject is diagrammed by splitting the subject line into a bracket and placing each individual subject on its own horizontal line of the bracket. Then, a vertical dotted line joins the horizontal lines, and the conjunction is placed on that dotted line.

Marcos and Carolina are making cookies with their mother.

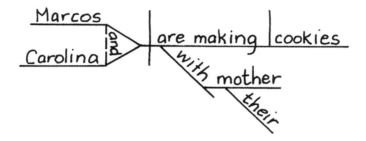

You may use an *x* to show that a comma has replaced a coordinating conjunction, but this is optional.

There, without a thought, she left the pathway, plunged into a field, and fell on the grass.*

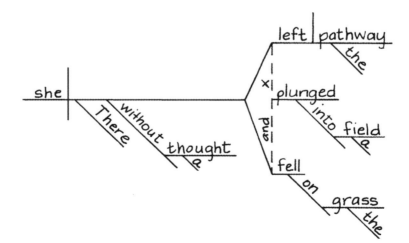

---

*adapted from *The Witch of Blackbird Pond* by Elizabeth George Speare

6. **Compound subjects with more than one coordinating conjunction**:
   When a sentence contains more than two subjects joined by more than
   one coordinating conjunction, place both conjunctions inside the
   bracket on the dotted line.

   The <u>horse</u> and the <u>hound</u> and the <u>horn</u> <u>belonged</u> to the farmer
   sowing his corn.

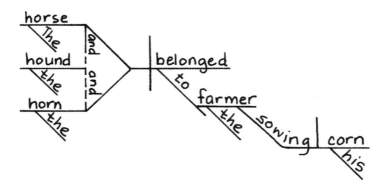

7. **Proper nouns** as subjects: When a proper noun with more than one
   word is a subject, whether it is a person's name, the title of a book, or the
   name of a ship or airplane, the words of the proper noun are not split up
   but are placed together on the subject line of the diagram.

   <u>Lady Sparrow</u> <u>was</u> with her family.*

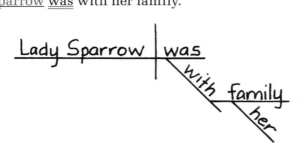

---

*adapted from *Japanese Fairy Tales* by Yei Theodora Ozaki

The *North Star* <u>made</u> her way into a small inlet in the ice.

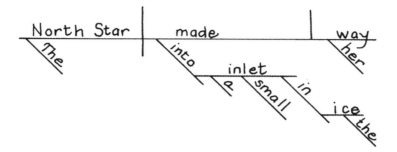

8. **Indefinite pronouns** as subjects: An indefinite pronoun (a pronoun without an antecedent) can be a subject and is placed on the subject line of the diagram.

<u>Someone</u> <u>was dragging</u> a chain.*

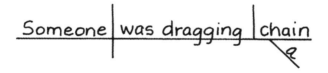

9. **Prepositional phrases** as subjects: A subject can never be found inside of a prepositional phrase, but an entire prepositional phrase can serve as a subject. It is diagrammed on a pedestal on the subject line of the sentence, with any modifiers of the phrase attached to it.

<u>Under the bridge</u> <u>is</u> not a safe place.

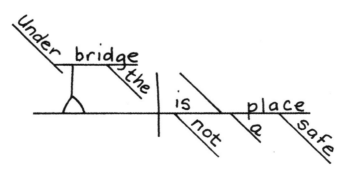

---

*adapted from *A Christmas Carol* by Charles Dickens

10. **Demonstrative pronouns** as subjects: A demonstrative pronoun can act as the subject of a sentence, and if it is acting as the subject, it is placed on the subject line.

This tastes delectable.

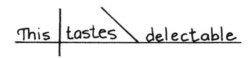

11. **Interrogative pronouns** as subjects: An interrogative pronoun can act as the subject of a sentence, and if it is acting as the subject, it is placed on the subject line.

Who made you the judge of your brother?

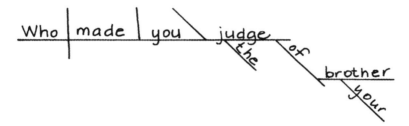

12. **Contractions** as subjects: When a subject is part of a contraction, put only the pronoun part of the contraction on the subject line.

I've almost broken my neck.*

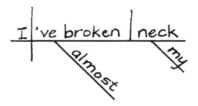

---

*adapted from *Rebecca of Sunnybrook Farm* by Kate Douglas Wiggin

13. **Intensive pronouns** with a subject: When an intensive pronoun is adding intensity to a subject, diagram it in parentheses after the subject to demonstrate that it is a non-essential element in the sentence.

> The three inner <u>satellites</u> themselves <u>are eclipsed</u> by the shadow of Jupiter.

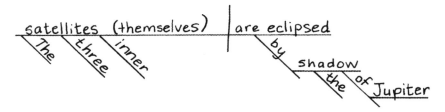

14. **Gerunds** as subjects: A gerund acting as a subject is placed on a pedestal on the subject line. It is diagrammed on a broken line to show that it is both noun and verb.

> <u>Galloping</u> <u>exhausted</u> the little mare.

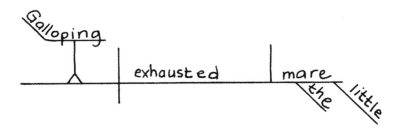

15. **Infinitives** as subjects: An infinitive acting as the subject is placed on a pedestal on the subject line. It is diagrammed on a broken line to show that it is both noun and verb.

> <u>To give</u> <u>is</u> to receive.

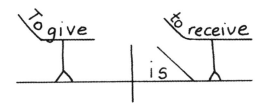

16. Compound subjects with **coordinating correlative conjunctions**: A
correlative conjunction joining compound subjects is diagrammed just
as a coordinating conjunction, except an ellipsis is used to connect the
conjunctions on the joining line.

In the beginning, both the <u>Sun</u> and the <u>Moon</u> <u>were</u> dark.

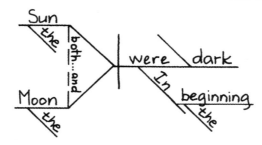

17. Appositive nouns after subjects: When diagramming an appositive
noun, place it in parentheses after the noun it renames or explains.

Rome's first <u>ruler</u>, Romulus, <u>killed</u> his brother and <u>seized</u> power.

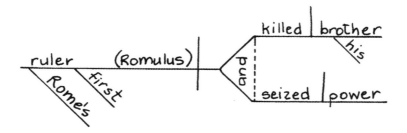

18. Unknown subjects with hortative verbs: Hortative sentences that use *let*
are often assigning the action to an unknown subject. Mark the subject
line with an *x* to indicate an unknown subject.

<u>Let</u> us travel safely.

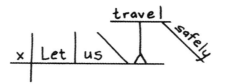

IB. Simple predicates

1. **Helping verbs:** Put any helping verbs next to the main verb on the predicate line. There may be more than one helping verb.

Other <u>animals</u> <u>were gathering</u> around.[*]

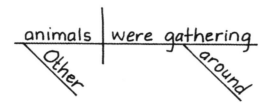

By that time, <u>they</u> <u>will have learned</u> their lesson.[†]

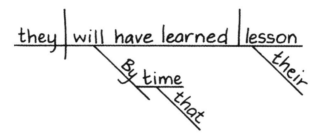

2. **Compound predicates:** A compound predicate consists of two or more verbs joined by a conjunction. Compound predicates are diagrammed by splitting the predicate line into a bracket after the subject/predicate dividing line. Each predicate is placed on its own horizontal line of the bracket. Then, a vertical dotted line joins the horizontal lines, and the conjunction is placed on that dotted line.

<u>Marcos</u> <u>adds</u> and <u>stirs</u> the ingredients.

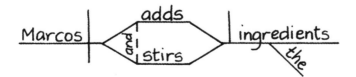

---

[*]adapted from "The Day Baboon Outwitted Leopard," as told by Nick Greaves in *When Hippo Was Hairy: And Other Tales from Africa*

[†]from *The Light Princess and Other Fairy Stories* by George MacDonald

3. Compound predicates with more than one coordinating conjunction:
When a sentence contains more than two predicates joined by more
than one coordinating conjunction, place both conjunctions inside the
bracket on the dotted line. You may use an *x* to show that a comma has
replaced a coordinating conjunction, but this is optional.

Sid <u>yawned</u>, <u>stretched</u>, and then <u>brought</u> himself up on his elbow
with a snort and <u>stared</u> at Tom.[*]

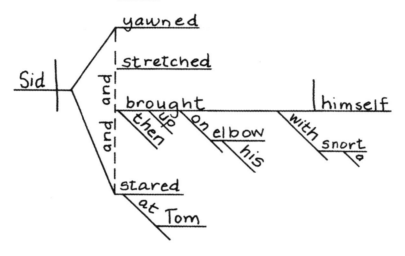

4. Contractions as predicates: When diagramming a contracted verb, place
only the contracted portion of the verb in the predicate space.

<u>It's</u> not there.

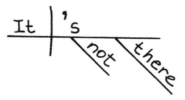

---

[*]from *The Adventures of Tom Sawyer* by Mark Twain

5. **The understood helping verb:** When a sentence contains two or more main verbs and one helping verb that applies to all of the main verbs, designate the understood helping verb with an *x*.

A <u>mist</u> of fine snowflakes <u>was curling</u> and <u>eddying</u> about the cluster of low drab buildings huddled on the grey prairies.*

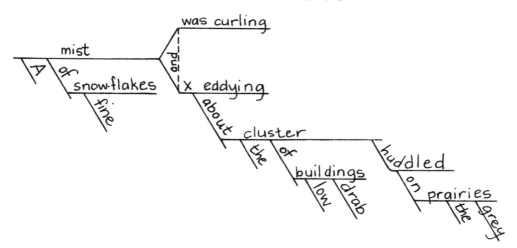

6. **Quasi-coordinators joining compound predicates:** Diagram quasi-coordinators on a horizontal dotted line between the words they connect.

<u>I</u> <u>will starve</u> rather than <u>eat</u> pistachio.

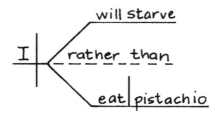

---

*adapted from *O Pioneers!* by Willa Cather

PART II: HOW TO DIAGRAM ADJECTIVES AND ADVERBS

IIA. Adjectives

1. **Descriptive adjectives:** Diagram a descriptive adjective on a slanted line underneath the word it is modifying.

A colossal, billowing <u>storm-cloud</u> <u>threatened</u>.[*]

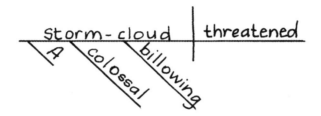

2. **Compound adjectives (single adjectives made up of more than one word):** A compound adjective, like a compound noun, goes on a single line and includes any hyphen (if present).

An iron-plated <u>monster</u> <u>had arisen</u>.[†]

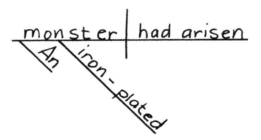

---

[*]adapted from *Twenty Thousand Leagues Under the Sea* by Jules Verne
[†]adapted from *Twenty Thousand Leagues Under the Sea* by Jules Verne

3. **Articles:** Like other adjectives, articles (*a, an, the*) are diagrammed on slanted lines beneath the nouns they describe.

The Rainbow's Daughter and the Rose Princess approached them.[*]

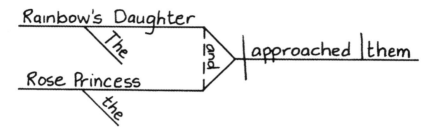

4. **Compound adjectives (two or more adjectives modifying the same noun):** When two adjectives modify the same noun and are linked by *and*, they are diagrammed on slanted lines underneath the noun they modify, and the conjunction is written on a dotted line linking the two adjectives together.

Tall and wide arches weren't often built.

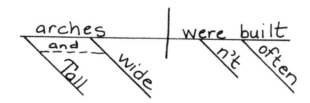

5. **Possessive pronouns as adjectives:** When a possessive pronoun is being used as a possessive adjective, it is diagrammed on a slanted line under the word it modifies.

Her cordial healed Edmund.[†]

cordial | healed | Edmund
  Her

[*]from *Tik-Tok of Oz* by L. Frank Baum
[†]adapted from *The Lion, The Witch, and the Wardrobe* by C. S. Lewis

6. **Indefinite pronouns acting as adjectives**: When an indefinite pronoun is being used as an adjective, it is placed on a slanted line under the word it modifies.

Many <u>guests</u> <u>arrived</u> early.

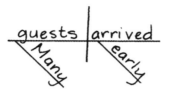

7. **Demonstrative pronouns as adjectives:** When a demonstrative pronoun (*this, that, these, those*) is used as an adjective, it is placed on a slanted line under the word it modifies.

<u>Mrs. Merriweather</u> <u>was</u> one of those childless adults.*

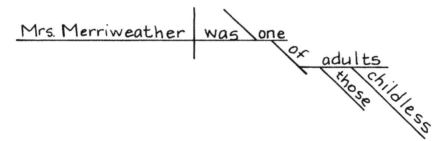

8. **Interrogative pronouns as adjectives:** The interrogative pronouns *whose, what,* and *which* can also be used as adjectives. They are diagrammed like other adjectives, on a slanted line under the word they are modifying.

Whose <u>blanket</u> <u>is</u> missing?

---

*from *To Kill A Mockingbird* by Harper Lee

9. Past participles as adjectives: When the past participle of a verb acts as a descriptive adjective, it is placed on a slanted line beneath the noun it modifies. However, the slanted line must curve around and become straight. Since adjectives are diagrammed on slanted lines, and verbs are diagrammed on straight lines, this type of line shows that the past participle has both adjective qualities and verb qualities.

The burst <u>balloon</u> <u>fit</u> inside the honey jar.

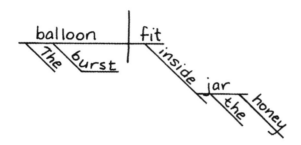

10. Present participles as adjectives: When the present participle of a verb acts as a descriptive adjective, it is placed on a slanted line beneath the noun it modifies. However, the slanted line must curve around and become straight. Since adjectives are diagrammed on slanted lines, and verbs are diagrammed on straight lines, this type of line shows that the present participle has both adjective qualities and verb qualities.

The snoring <u>guards</u> <u>lay</u> at the doorstep, fast asleep.

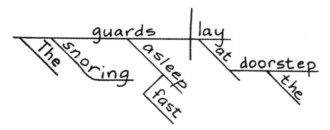

IIB. Adverbs

1. **Adverbs that modify verbs:** An adverb goes on a slanted line beneath the verb it modifies.

They rested peacefully.

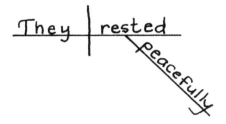

2. **Adverbs that modify adjectives:** An adverb that describes an adjective goes on a diagonal line underneath the adjective it modifies.

Extremely skittish Larry ran away.

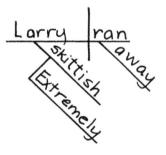

3. **Adverbs that modify other adverbs:** An adverb that describes another adverb goes on a diagonal line underneath the adverb it modifies.

Larry shrieked especially loudly.

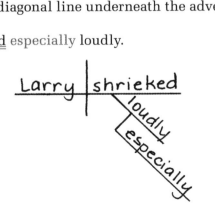

4. **Compound adverbs (two or more adverbs modifying the same word):**
When two adverbs modify the same word and are linked by *and*, they
are diagrammed on slanted lines underneath the word they modify,
and the conjunction is written on a dotted line linking the two adverbs
together.

The idea <u>was</u> deeply and widely <u>held</u>.

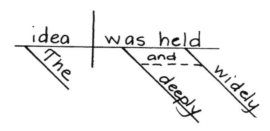

5. **Interrogative pronouns as adverbs:** When interrogative pronouns
answer the adverb questions (*where, when, how, how often, to what
extent*), they are diagrammed as adverbs, on a slanted line under the
verb(s) they are modifying.

Where <u>are</u> <u>you</u>?

6. **Adverbs of affirmation:** Adverbs such as *yes, surely, definitely, certainly,
absolutely,* and *very* make positive statements more affirming. They are
diagrammed on a slanted line under the word or words they modify.

Yes, I <u>will paint</u> you, Juanico.[*]

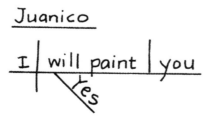

---

[*]from *I, Juan de Pareja* by Elizabeth Borton de Treviño

7. Adverbs of negation: The words *no, not,* and *never* can be used as adverbs of negation, stating what is not true or does not exist. They are diagrammed on a slanted line under the word or words they modify. When they are used as part of a contraction, they are diagrammed with only the contracted portion of the word on the slanted line.

You will never be beaten again.*

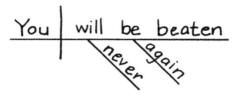

It doesn't matter.

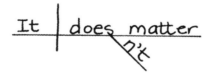

*from *I, Juan de Pareja* by Elizabeth Borton de Treviño

PART III: HOW TO DIAGRAM PREPOSITIONAL PHRASES

IIIA. Prepositional phrases acting as modifiers

1. **Prepositional phrases that act as adjectives:** Prepositional phrases that modify nouns or pronouns are diagrammed underneath the word or words they modify. The preposition is placed on a diagonal line, the object of the preposition is placed on a horizontal line, and any adjectives modifying the object go on diagonal lines underneath the object.

Caleb climbed a tree with thick branches.

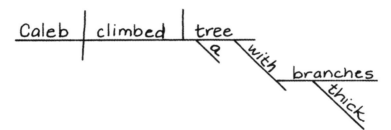

2. **Prepositional phrases that act as predicate adjectives:** A prepositional phrase can act as an adjective describing the subject. It is diagrammed after the slanted line, following the linking verb, and it is placed on a pedestal. The preposition is put on a diagonal line, the object of the preposition is on a horizontal line, and any modifiers are placed on a diagonal line underneath the object.

The man is in love.

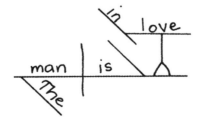

21

3. **Prepositional phrases modifying other prepositional phrases:** When a prepositional phrase is acting as an adjective or adverb, it can sometimes be modified by another prepositional phrase. The second phrase is diagrammed below the first.

Smaller <u>objects</u> near the horizon <u>might influence</u> our ideas about the size of the moon.

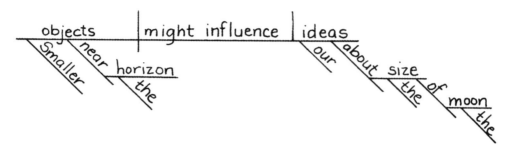

4. **Prepositional phrases that act as adverbs:** When a prepositional phrase answers one of the questions *how, when, where, how often, to what extent*, it is an adverb phrase. It is diagrammed under the verb, adjective, or adverb that it modifies. The preposition is placed on a diagonal line, the object of the preposition is placed on a horizontal line, and any adjectives modifying the object go on diagonal lines underneath the object.

<u>Hank Aaron</u> <u>swung</u> the bat through the air with great confidence.

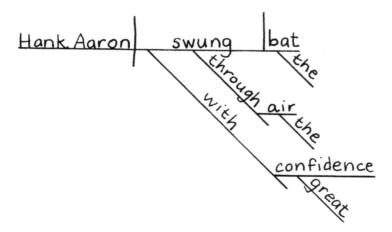

IIIB. Prepositional phrases acting as nouns

1. Prepositional phrases that act as subjects: When the prepositional phrase acts as the subject, it is diagrammed on a pedestal on the subject line.

Under the bridge is not a safe place.

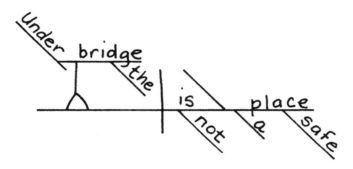

2. Prepositional phrases that act as direct objects: When the prepositional phrase receives the action of the verb, it is acting as a direct object. It is diagrammed on a pedestal on a horizontal line, and it is placed after the action verb. A vertical line is drawn between the verb and the object. However, the vertical line stops at the horizontal line and does not go through.

Rann had never seen Mowgli before, though of course he had heard of him.*

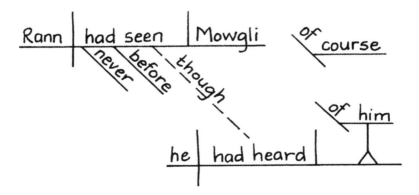

---

*from *The Jungle Book* by Rudyard Kipling

3. Prepositional phrases that act as predicate nominatives: When the prepositional phrase renames the subject, it is acting as a predicate nominative. It is diagrammed on a pedestal on a horizontal line, and it is placed after the linking verb and a slanted line pointing back to the subject.

The best <u>place</u> for the treasure <u>is</u> under the bed.

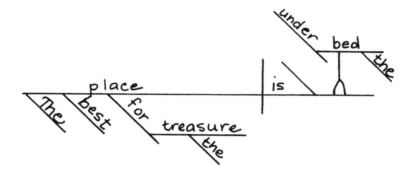

4. Prepositional phrases that act as objects of the preposition: Sometimes a prepositional phrase acts as an object of the preposition. It is diagrammed on a pedestal on the horizontal line where the object of the preposition is normally placed.

<u>He</u> <u>stepped</u> from behind the tree.

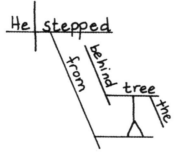

IIIC. Objects of prepositions, special cases

1. **Compound objects of prepositions:** A prepositional phrase may contain more than one object of the preposition. In this case, the objects are compound, and are diagrammed as any other compound element. The objects line is split into a bracket, the objects are written on separate horizontal lines, and the conjunction joining them is placed on the dotted line.

The <u>gratin</u> of potato and cheese <u>smelled</u> absolutely delightful.

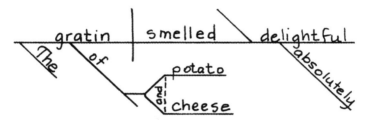

2. **Gerunds as objects of prepositions:** A gerund can function as the object of the preposition. In this case, the gerund is diagrammed on the horizontal object line, but it is placed on a pedestal and written on a curved line, in order to demonstrate that it is a combination of both noun and verb.

The <u>Giant</u> <u>was tired</u> of working.*

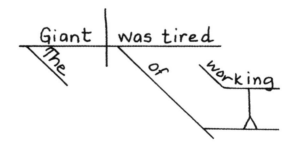

---

*adapted from *Myths of the Norsemen from the Eddas and Sagas* by H. A. Guerber

PART IV: OBJECTS

IVA. Direct objects

1. **Direct objects:** Usually, a direct object is a noun or pronoun receiving the action of the verb. It is diagrammed on the horizontal line after the action verb, and a vertical line is placed between the verb and the object. However, the vertical line stops at the horizontal line and does not go through (this differentiates the direct object line from the subject/verb dividing line).

We <u>roasted</u> marshmallows.

We | roasted | marshmallows

2. **Compound direct objects:** When a sentence contains more than one direct object, the objects are diagrammed like any other compound element. The horizontal line is split into a bracket, and the objects are each placed on separate horizontal lines with a dotted line joining them. The vertical direct object line is placed on the horizontal line before the bracket, in order to indicate that the compound elements are direct objects.

<u>We</u> <u>roasted</u> soft marshmallows and beefy hot dogs.

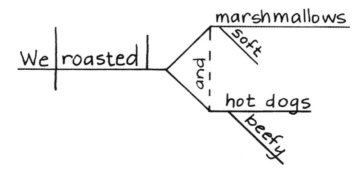

3. Compound predicates with compound direct objects: When a sentence
contains more than one verb, and each verb has its own direct object(s),
the verbs are placed on a bracket to indicate a compound element,
and the direct objects are put after the verb(s) whose action they are
receiving.

The Dragon King with his retainers <u>accompanied</u> the warrior to the
end of the bridge, and <u>took</u> leave of him with many bows and good
wishes.

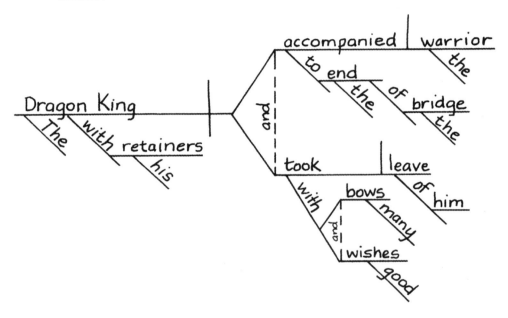

4. Compound predicates with the same direct object: When a sentence
contains more than one verb, and the verbs share the same direct object,
the verbs are placed on a bracket to indicate a compound element. The
brackets then rejoin, a direct object line is placed on the horizontal line,
and the direct object goes after the verbs.

In the bakery, <u>I</u> <u>see</u> and <u>smell</u> my favorite things.

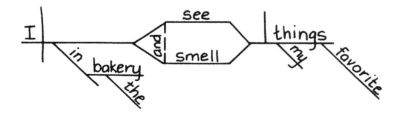

5. **Interrogative pronouns as direct objects:** Interrogative pronouns can be used as direct objects in a sentence. They are diagrammed just as regular direct objects would be.

He <u>did</u> what?

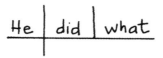

6. **Demonstrative pronouns as direct objects:** Demonstrative pronouns (*this*, *that*, *these*, *those*) can be direct objects and are diagrammed just as regular direct objects would be.

<u>Who</u> <u>brought</u> this?

7. **Gerunds as direct objects:** When a gerund is a direct object, it is placed on a pedestal on the horizontal direct object line. The line it is on is curved to demonstrate that the gerund is part noun and part verb.

<u>Loki</u> <u>heard</u> flapping.*

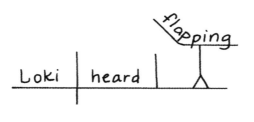

*adapted from *Myths of the Norsemen from the Eddas and Sagas* by H.A. Guerber

8. **Infinitives as direct objects:** When an infinitive is a direct object, it is placed on a pedestal on the horizontal line and after the vertical direct object line. Its line is curved to demonstrate that the infinitive is part noun and part verb.

The old <u>soldier</u> <u>did</u> not <u>fear</u> to die.

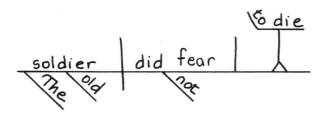

9. **Compound nouns or proper names as direct objects:** When a compound noun or proper name is used as a direct object, the words are not split up. The entire noun or name is placed on the direct object line.

<u>Thomas Jefferson</u>, <u>who</u> <u>was</u> the third President of the United States, <u>built</u> the University of Virginia.

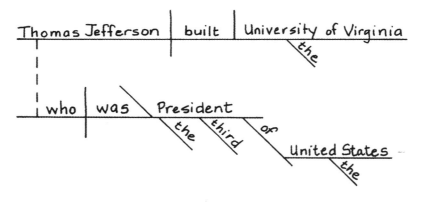

10. **Understood direct object:** When a sentence contains an understood direct object (such as an understood relative pronoun), an *x* is placed in the direct object location of the diagram.

   This <u>is</u> the house <u>Jack</u> <u>built</u>. (The understood relative pronoun *that* is represented by the *x*).

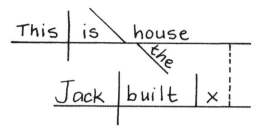

11. **Appositive nouns after direct objects:** When an appositive noun renames or explains a direct object, it is placed in parentheses after the direct object on the diagram.

   <u>They</u> <u>heard</u> with terror the advancing drums, the sound of doom.

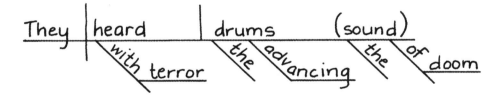

12. **Object complements:** When a noun follows the direct object and renames it, it is an object complement noun. It is diagrammed on a horizontal line after the direct object, and a slanted line is placed between the direct object and the object complement to indicate that the complement is renaming the object.

   The <u>group</u> <u>elected</u> you president.

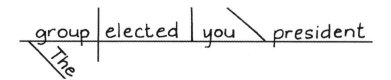

When an adjective follows the direct object and describes that object, it is called an object complement adjective and is diagrammed the same way.

The <u>instructor</u> <u>found</u> the students intelligent.

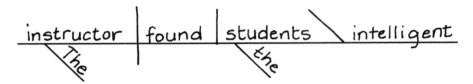

IVB. Indirect objects

1. **Indirect objects:** The indirect object is written underneath the verb on a horizontal line. It connects to the verb by a slanted line, but nothing is written on the slanted line. That slanted line is a reminder that the verb indirectly affects the indirect object.

   <u>Odysseus</u> <u>asked</u> the stranger a question.*

   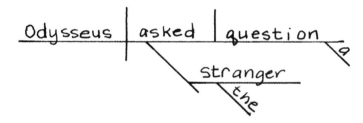

2. **Compound indirect objects:** When a sentence contains a compound indirect object, both indirect objects are placed on horizontal lines drawn as a bracket. The conjunction is placed on the dotted line, and the entire structure is joined to the sentence on a slanted line attached underneath the verb.

---

*from *The Odyssey* by Homer

Brandon <u>sent</u> his cousin and uncle an email.

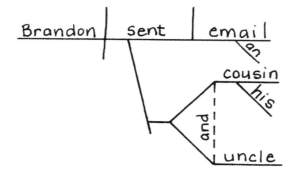

3. **Proper nouns as indirect objects:** When a proper noun such as a name or title is used as an indirect object, the entire noun is placed on the indirect object line. No part of the proper noun is used as a modifier.

<u>I</u> <u>knitted</u> Aunt Judy the mittens.

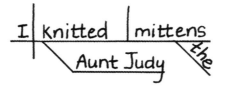

PART V: PREDICATE ADJECTIVES AND PREDICATE NOMINATIVES

VA. Predicate adjectives

1. **Predicate adjective:** A predicate adjective is diagrammed by placing it on the horizontal line after the linking verb. Between the verb and the predicate adjective, a slanted line is drawn that points back to the subject, demonstrating the function of the predicate adjective (a word modifying the subject).

I <u>am</u> unpopular.

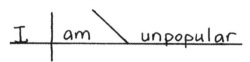

2. **Compound predicate adjectives:** When a sentence contains more than one predicate adjective, the horizontal predicate line is divided into a bracket after the linking verb and after the slanted line pointing back to the subject. Each adjective is placed on a separate horizontal line, and the conjunction joining the adjectives is drawn on the dotted line of the bracket.

Bat <u>caves</u> <u>can be</u> dark and creepy.

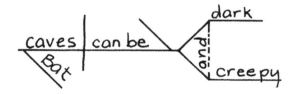

3. **Prepositional phrases as predicate adjectives:** When a prepositional phrase is used as a predicate adjective, the entire phrase is placed on a pedestal following the linking verb and the slanted line pointing back to the subject. Any modifiers are put on slanted lines beneath the word or words they modify, but still on the pedestal, not underneath the sentence's horizontal line.

The <u>waiters</u> <u>are</u> in elaborate green uniforms.

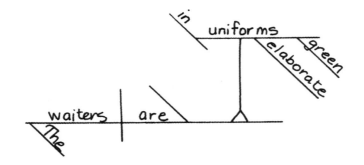

VB. Predicate nominatives

1. **Predicate nominatives:** A predicate nominative is diagrammed by placing it on the horizontal line after the linking verb. Between the verb and the predicate nominative, a slanted line is drawn, pointing back to the subject and demonstrating the function of the predicate nominative (a word renaming the subject).

I <u>am</u> a berry.

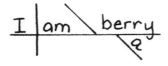

2. Compound predicate nominatives: When a sentence contains more than one predicate nominative, the horizontal predicate line is split into a bracket after the linking verb and the slanted line pointing back to the subject. Each adjective is placed on a separate horizontal line, and the conjunction joining the nominatives is written on the dotted line of the bracket.

The <u>persons</u> still in the tavern <u>were</u> a man <u>who</u> <u>appeared</u> to be an artisan, drunk, but not extremely so, sitting before a pot of beer, and his companion, a huge, stout man with a grey beard.

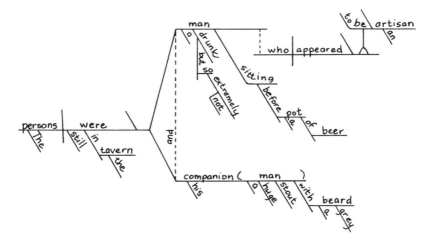

3. Infinitives as predicate nominatives: An infinitive predicate nominative is diagrammed by placing it on a pedestal on the main subject-predicate line, but after the slanted line pointing to the subject. All modifiers are written on slanted lines under the word or words they modify, but still on the pedestal, not on the main horizontal line of the sentence.

To <u>exist</u> <u>is</u> to change.

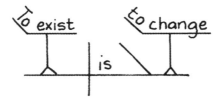

PART VI: PHRASES AND CLAUSES

We have already covered prepositional phrases, but there are several other types of phrases and clauses that can function as essential parts of the sentence. Their diagrams are demonstrated in this section.

VIA. Phrases

1. **Verb Phrases:** A verb phrase includes the main verb of the sentence and all of its helping verbs. When diagramming a verb phrase, all of the helping verbs are placed next to the main verb on the horizontal line.

By that time, <u>they</u> <u>will have learned</u> their lesson.*

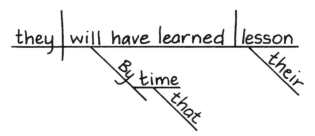

---

*from *The Light Princess and Other Fairy Stories* by George MacDonald

39

2. **Gerund, participle, and infinitive phrases as direct objects:** A gerund (present participle acting as a noun), participle, or infinitive and all of the words that go with it form a gerund phrase, participle phrase, or infinitive phrase. The phrase is diagrammed according to its function in the sentence. When it is acting as the direct object, it is placed after the direct object line. The entire phrase is elevated on a pedestal to demonstrate that it is a phrase and not a typical direct object. The gerund, participle, or infinitive phrase may contain its own objects and modifiers, and they are included on the pedestal as well, diagrammed in their appropriate spots.

I <u>love</u> eating pancakes with maple syrup, yellow cake with chocolate frosting, and grilled ribeye steaks.

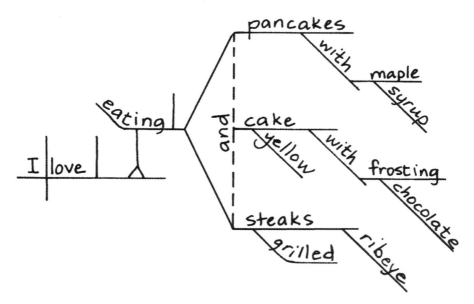

3. **Gerund and infinitive phrases as subjects:** When a gerund or infinitive phrase is acting as the subject of the sentence, it is placed on the subject line. The entire phrase is elevated on a pedestal to demonstrate that it is a phrase and not a typical subject. The gerund or infinitive phrase may contain its own objects and modifiers, and they are included on the pedestal as well, diagrammed in their appropriate spots.

<u>Lighting</u> by means of gas <u>was</u> yet <u>unknown</u>.*

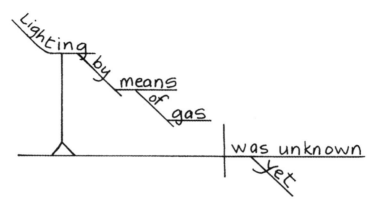

---

*from *Stories of Great Inventors* by H.E. Macomber

4. Gerund and infinitive phrases as predicate nominatives: A gerund or infinitive phrase may act as the predicate nominative of the sentence. In this case, it is diagrammed after the linking verb and the slanted line dividing the verb from the predicate nominative. The entire phrase is elevated on a pedestal to demonstrate that it is a verbal phrase and not a typical predicate nominative. The gerund or infinitive phrase may contain its own objects and modifiers, and they are included on the pedestal as well, diagrammed in their appropriate spots.

I was to wait for arms and armor to aid me.[*]

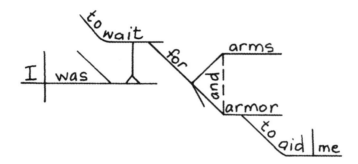

5. Participle and infinitive phrases as predicate adjectives: Phrases serving as predicate adjectives are diagrammed after the linking verb and the slanted line dividing the verb from the predicate adjective. The entire phrase is elevated on a pedestal to demonstrate that it is a phrase and not a typical subject complement. The phrase may contain its own objects and modifiers, and they are included on the pedestal as well, diagrammed in their appropriate spots.

Were they not broken of heart?[†]

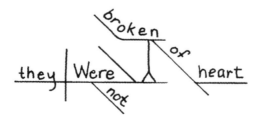

[*]from *The Story of the Champions of the Round Table* by Howard Pyle
[†]from *The Story of the Champions of the Round Table* by Howard Pyle

VIB. Independent clauses

1. **Multiple independent clauses:** When a sentence contains more than one independent clause, the clauses are diagrammed on separate horizontal lines and are joined by a dotted line connecting the predicates of the clauses. A shelf for the conjunction joining the clauses is placed in the middle of the dotted line, and if there is no conjunction, an *x* is placed on the shelf.

Mr. Collins <u>was</u> not agreeable; his <u>society</u> <u>was</u> irksome, and his <u>attachment</u> to her <u>must be</u> imaginary.[*]

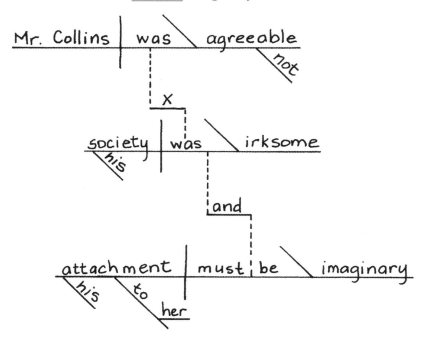

---

[*]from *Pride and Prejudice* by Jane Austen

VIC. Dependent clauses

1. **Dependent clauses acting as adjectives:** When a dependent clause is an adjective clause, the independent clause containing it is diagrammed first. Then, the adjective clause is placed underneath the independent clause, and a dotted line is used to connect the noun or pronoun in the independent clause to the adjective clause that is modifying it. If a relative pronoun is being used, the dotted line connects the relative pronoun to the noun or pronoun being modified. If a relative adverb is being used, the dotted line connects the relative adverb to the noun or pronoun it is modifying.

Relative adjective example:

I <u>who</u> <u>speak</u> to you <u>have seen</u> many evils.

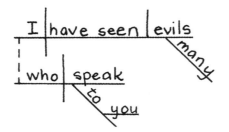

Relative adverb example:

The <u>sea</u> <u>is</u> a green pasture where our children's <u>grand-children</u> <u>will</u> <u>go</u> for bread.*

---

*from *Moby Dick*, by Herman Melville

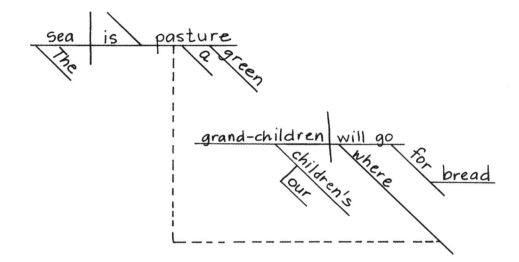

2. **Dependent clauses acting as adverbs:** When a dependent clause is an adverb clause, the independent clause containing it is diagrammed first. Then, the adverb clause is placed underneath the independent clause, and a dotted line is used to connect the the adverb clause to the word that it modifies. The dotted line begins at the verb, adjective, or adverb being modified by the adverb clause, and ends at the verb in the adverb clause itself.

When the supper <u>was finished</u>, the king <u>expressed</u> a wish.

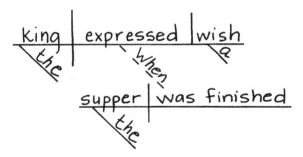

3. **Dependent clauses acting as nouns:** A noun clause can have any function in a sentence that a noun would have. It can be a subject, direct object, indirect object, predicate nominative, or object of the preposition. When a noun clause is diagrammed, it is placed on a pedestal to demonstrate that it is not a one-word sentence element attached to the clause's predicate. If the clause contains its own modifiers and objects, those are placed in the appropriate spots on the pedestal.

Noun clause as subject:

Whatever had seized him made snorting noises.*

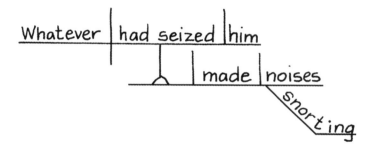

Noun clause as direct object:

I know where your lost keys are.

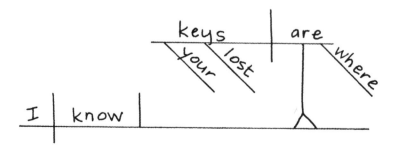

---

*from *The Book of Three* by Lloyd Alexander

Noun clause as predicate nominative:

<u>What was best about flying any of the kites</u> <u>was</u> what it <u>did</u> for Mother.[*]

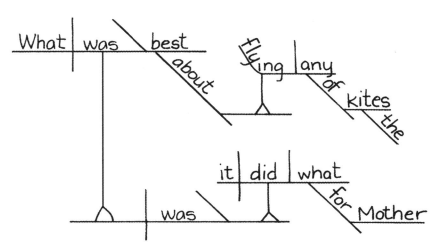

Noun clause as object of the preposition: If *that* is acting as a subordinating word, rather than as a demonstrative pronoun, it should be placed on a horizontal line above the predicate, connected to the predicate with a dotted vertical line.

I have previously written about how much we are affected by atmospheres here, and I think that in my own case this trouble is getting much worse lately.*

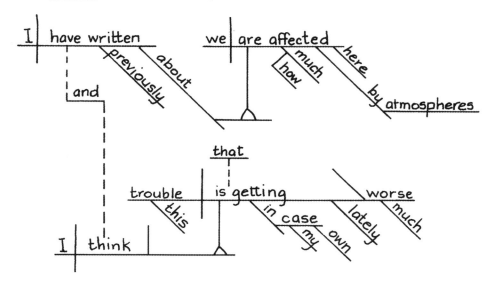

---

*from Anne Frank's *The Diary of a Young Girl* translated from the Dutch by B.M. Mooyart

Noun clause as appositive: When a dependent noun clause acts as an appositive, the entire noun clause is placed on a tree in the appositive space, between parentheses.

The article's <u>argument</u>, that <u>studying</u> grammar <u>is</u> good for your brain, <u>didn't</u> <u>convince</u> me.

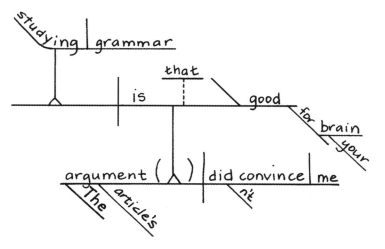

PART VII: FILLING UP THE CORNERS

1. **Parenthetical elements:** When a parenthetical element is not connected to the sentence in any grammatical way, it is diagrammed off to the side or underneath the sentence, to show that it belongs to the sentence but has no grammatical connection to the sentence.

We <u>met</u> the new neighbors today, <u>who</u>, <u>we think</u>, <u>are</u> very pleasant people.

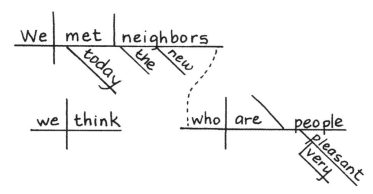

The <u>train</u>—<u>can you believe</u> it?—<u>was</u> on time (a rare and happy occurrence).

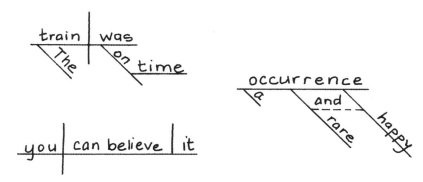

2. **Noun of direct address:** A noun of direct address names a person or thing who is being spoken to. It is diagrammed on a separate line above the diagram to demonstrate its lack of grammatical connection to the sentence.

Friends, Romans, countrymen, <u>lend</u> me your ears!

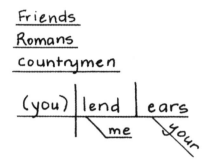

3. **Interjection:** An interjection is diagrammed on a free-floating line above the sentence, to show that it does not have a clear grammatical connection to the sentence.

Whew! <u>That</u> <u>was</u> a close one.

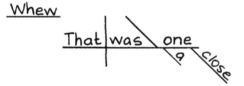

4. **Phrases as appositives:** When a phrase acts as an appositive, only the appositive noun is placed in parentheses after the word it renames or explains. Any modifiers are placed beneath the appositive noun.

Chinese tin <u>miners</u> <u>founded</u> the Malaysian city Kuala Lumpur, the Golden Triangle, in 1857.

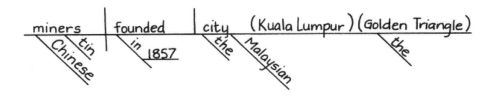

5. **Absolute constructions:** An absolute construction has a strong semantic relationship to the sentence, but no grammatical relationship to it. Like parenthetical elements, absolute constructions are diagrammed separately from the main sentence. Absolute constructions are diagrammed above the sentence to demonstrate that they are more important to the sentence than a parenthetical element is.

<u>Dr. Bauerstein</u> <u>remained</u> in the background, his grave bearded face unchanged.*

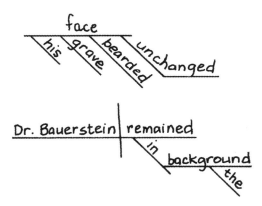

---

*from *The Mysterious Affair at Styles* by Agatha Christie

INDEX